30 DAYS IN THE DESERT

Christina L. Walls

PREFACE

A desert is a naturally harsh and dry land, one that seems to not offer much hope. Yet oftentimes I have found that on life's journey with the Lord we will pass through many deserts and dry lands to get us where God wants us to be. The harsh elements will either consume us and we will lie down and give up while in the desert, or we will find the strength the Lord provides to carry us through the desert into his desired destination. *30 Days in the Desert* is a simple look into the journey and the treasures that I discovered while passing through the desert. I have learned that adversity will strengthen us a million times more than a road of comfort if we allow it to and refuse to give up.

INTRODUCTION

Behold, I will do a new thing; now it shall
spring forth and you shall know it. I will even
make a way in the wilderness and rivers in the
desert.

—Isaiah 43:19

Many times in life we are faced with situations
we never imagined we would have to encounter. Life
can seem to throw many punches our way and we are
left sometimes facing choices that seem difficult. But
with every circumstance and situation we are given a
choice on how we will respond. We cannot always
control or predict what goes on around us, but God has
given us a way of escape if we chose to take it. Many
times we try to make our own way and end up

frustrated and discouraged, but when we take ourselves and all of our circumstances to Jesus, we cannot go wrong. It doesn't mean he will step in and make everything just perfect according to how we may want it; however, if we are willing to give it up and surrender it to him, he will make it perfect according to his will and eternal plan.

His will may not always feel the best at the time and may require waiting through times that seem impossible and through trials that you would rather avoid altogether. His will may take you through humiliating paths and down roads that seem unending. Yet if we truly take the time to draw near to the Savior and seek his will and him, he will work everything out for us when it's all said and done. We will look back, if we stay the course and keep our faith in him, and see how all through our trials he was doing a great work within us and for us. His concern is not so much our comfort as much as it is our eternal destination. He told us in this life we would have trials and difficulties but through them all we are to keep praising and serving the Most High God, who loves us and cares for us more than we can imagine.

So in these few pages I hope to share with you from my personal experiences and lessons the Lord has shared with me as I have walked with him. I have to admit the path seemed too difficult sometimes and honestly at times it was, but he always showed up, maybe not the way I had expected but in the way I needed. Some things I never want to go through again because they were terribly painful, but I know had I been spared the pain, I would have never learned what

God wanted me to know and for that I am thankful.

Not all situations are perfectly smoothed out in my life;

I am still waiting on some things, I am still pressing on

in areas, I am still hoping, still trusting, and still

believing in a God that I know will not let me down.

LET THE WILD HORSE RUN

Let the wild horse run
Full stride through the woods
He falters not at the fallen trees
Nor withholds his strength
He charges on
His heart not weary
His power not compromised
He looks not at the obstacles
But presses on unaffected
For his goal lies ahead
And his steps are sure
If the storm comes he slows not his pace
Nor is affected by the wind and the rain
For his power is mighty and he fears not
The sword does not hinder his goal
He charges into the fray
The sound of the trumpet ignites his muscles
He forces his body to continue on
He is not prevented by terror or task
For he is well acquainted with his maker
And questions not his purpose nor his being
But rejoices in his endowment
Not willing to withhold what God has created in him
So let the wild horses run
Full stride through the woods
Fulfilling the call and purpose of their creator

FREEDOM AND VICTORY

Do you not know that the runners in a race all run, but only one is victorious? So you must run that you may obtain victory. And every man who battles in the contest frees his mind from everything else. And yet they run to win a garland which is perishable; but we to win one which is everlasting. I therefore so run, not for something that is uncertain; and I so fight, not as one who beats the air. But I conquer and subdue my body so that, by no chance, when I have preached to others, will I despise myself.

—1 Corinthians 9:24-27

This is such a great word of encouragement and motivation. We are to run the race as if to expect victory. We are to free our minds from everything that hinders that goal. So what is the goal? I believe it is simply Jesus and the Kingdom of God, a goal that is not perishable but everlasting. So many of us get so busy with so much, running here and there and never taking the time to see if what we are doing is God's will. We exhaust ourselves for perishable, worldly things. If our goals are rooted in this world all that exists on the exterior, then we will gain what the world has to offer and in doing so we forfeit God's will and plan for our lives. So many times we find our minds on our own lives, troubles, and goals and we become entangled in ourselves, much like a fly getting entangled in the spider's web.

The Bible tells us we are to keep our hearts and minds stayed on Jesus, therefore freeing our minds from all the cares, ambitions, fears, and desires of this world. We need to be free to obtain the victory. Paul tells us that he conquers and subdues his body (1 Corin. 9:27). He makes his body obey him rather than obeying the cravings and desires of his body. He practices self-control, a fruit of the Spirit. This is impossible to do when our minds are so occupied with the affairs of this world and ourselves. We need to stop and lay down our agendas and seek the Lord. Return to our first love. If we don't, one day we could wake up and it will be too late. We will have lived a life full of selfishness, self-centeredness, and self-ambition only to regret it eternally.

Freeing our minds will not only allow us to obtain the victory but it will allow us to be free indeed. Free to live the life we were created for, one that loves and serves the Living God. One that says, "Not my will, Oh Lord, but your will be done." A life surrendered to the will of the Father. We need to cut out the meaningless activities and question why we're doing what we do. Are your daily activities, drawing you closer to God? Could it even be nothing more than busyness with a "ministry" label attached to it? Did God tell you to do this or was it man or your own imagination? We need to be honest with ourselves and seek God on our daily lives.

The world runs and chases after the wind but I believe the people of God need to slow down and wait upon the Lord to speak to us before we step out. Why live a life in vain that gives no glory to God? Why sacrifice yourself for such unprofitable things? Hear the Lord calling you to return to Him: "Deny yourself, take up your cross and follow me. For whoever wishes to save his life will lose it; and whoever loses his life for my sake and the sake of my gospel will save it" (Mark 8:34-35). There really is no other way for a child of God.

I WILL BE WITH YOU

When you pass through the sea, I will be with you; and through the rivers, they shall not overwhelm you; when you walk through the fire, you shall not be burned; neither shall the flame kindle upon you. For I am the Lord your God, the Holy One of Israel, your Savior; I gave Egypt for your sake, and Ethiopia and Sheba for you. Because you are precious in my sight, you have been honorable and I have loved you; therefore I have given men for your sake and nations for your life.

—Isaiah 43:2-4

How great is our God and how worthy to be praised. He never promised we wouldn't face hard trials. He never said it would be easy. He never told us there would not be a cost. He has told us that through it all he would be with us. So many times we find ourselves in situations beyond our ability to do anything. We look around and ask, what am I to do? What is ahead? How do I deal with this? You may question yourself and wonder did I sin? Did I do something wrong? Why is this happening?

Oftentimes these difficult times are our greatest blessings. We are the gold being purified by the fire. If we do not run from the trial but rather submit to God, we will find these times, in spite of their great difficulty, to be precious times with the Lord. We will often feel closer to him and see his mighty hand move during these times. We usually spend more time with the Lord when the fire is hot and the weight is heavy.

Our trials do more for us spiritually than any mountain top ever could. In the valley or in the raging sea is where we surrender and let go, allowing God to work in us and for us. If taken with the right attitude and humility, the trial will prove to be our greatest reward. Embrace the times of hardship and willingly give yourself over to Jesus and he will lift you up. This is oftentimes the point in which a person either submits to God or runs. To run is to turn from the cross and refuse the life of Jesus and what a shame it is to deny that which we so desperately need.

THE WAITING

But they that wait upon the Lord shall renew their strength, they shall mount up with wings like eagles, they shall run and not be weary, they shall walk and not faint.

—Isaiah 40:31

In a world where we want everything instantly, being asked to wait can arouse a sense of frustration and discouragement. It can lead us to take matters into our own hands in our pathetic efforts to make something happen, only to end up right where we started or in a worse situation that now needs fixing. Waiting takes us down roads we really don't want to go. It takes us to a point of surrendering or giving up. It takes us to the end of our ideas, timing, efforts, manipulations, strengths, and even our dreams. We will have to pass through deprivation and disappointment perhaps for years until we let go of all that we hold on to that will ultimately harm us.

Most of the scriptures on waiting in the Bible also refer to taking courage and our strength being renewed; rightfully so, because the waiting will demand courage and strength as we pass through days and years hoping and seeking that which was promised to us. It will require faith far beyond what the eye can see as stated in the book of Hebrews 11:1, "Now faith is the substance of things hoped for and the evidence of things not seen."

Waiting will take us on a journey past this world and its impatient desires and striving. Waiting will move us to a place of contentment in God if we allow it to do its intended work. Waiting on God will allow us to praise and worship the Lord with no agenda, once the agenda has been laid at the feet of Jesus along with all of our anxious desires and wants. It will become a blessing and a matter that creates character within us by the hand of God.

However, I am aware that some will not wait and will take matters into their own hands, or they will abandon the course and pursue their own ideas only to end up far from God and his plan. Not waiting can cause marriages to end, ministries to fail, souls to remain in the balance, families to become damaged and broken, dreams to fall at the wayside, and it can cause lives to remain unchanged and promises unfulfilled. When we think we know best and refuse God's ways, we forfeit the creator's plan for our lives and are left with what the world has to offer; which is a rebel's portion and a mocker's reward.

Endure the path of waiting, count up the cost, and set your eyes on Jesus. Make up your mind to obey his plan and path for your life. I know it will be the best when it is all said and done: "Weeping may

14

endure for a night but joy comes in the morning"

(Psalm 30:5).

SEEK THE LORD

Seek ye first the Kingdom of God and his righteousness and all these things will be added unto you.

—Matthew 6:33

I find it interesting that there is a great idea floating around regarding finding your passion and fulfilling our purpose. Many seek what they are passionate about then pursue it as a career, and in doing so they promote this alone will bring satisfaction. I believe it to be a trick because as long as we are seeking our value and worth outside of Christ, we are essentially denying God as our master and assuming we can find life and meaning in a career or in a passion. Passion is usually based in emotions, feelings, and our ambitions rather than God. If God calls you to do something and you are passionate about it, then you're in agreement with God and his will. But when we follow emotions and selfish ambitions, we move away from God.

The world promotes following your dreams and reaching your goals and all of this is good if Jesus is truly the master of our lives; if he is not, then we seek in vain and end up with frustrating paths. I believe if we are willing to lay all of our ambitions, dreams, and goals aside and diligently seek God and his Kingdom, everything will fall into place in our lives. How can it not? If we are willing to seek God for our lives and really find out what he wants for us without "self" in the way, I believe this is the only way a Christian will ever know and have true peace and satisfaction.

How can we find peace and satisfaction when we are resisting God's kingdom? In seeking God we are promised to find him: "I love those who love me and those who seek me diligently find me" (Prov. 8:17). We usually seek after what we love and pursue it. When a man loves a woman he seeks after her, in hope he can pursue and attain her love in return. As Christians, our purpose is not in things, careers, ambitions, relationships, fortune, or fame, but in the pursuit and attainment of knowing God. This alone will satisfy our hearts and minds and cause us to receive all that God has for us.

Seeking is not passive; it requires effort. We cannot go day after day ignoring God in prayer, neglecting to seek him in his word. If our lives are so busy we don't have time to really seek God but rather we merely get down in prayer out of guilt and obligation, then we are not really seeking God; we are just trying to justify ourselves. We need to make the choice to make time to seek God. Nothing in this world is so important that it takes us away from seeking God; we need to evaluate our lives and take control of the way we spend our time. Seek God wholeheartedly until you want to be alone with God and you would prefer spending time with him rather than doing other meaningless things. He needs to be more important than whatever else you are chasing after. Until we make him the priority, he will not be found by us and we do not want to miss him; nothing in this world is more important than our relationship with Jesus.

A TIME TO REPENT

But if a wicked man turns away from all the sins he has committed and keeps all my decrees and does what is just and right, he will surely live; he will not die. None of the offenses he has committed will be remembered against him. Because of the righteous things he has done, he will live. "Do I take any pleasure in the death of the wicked?" Declares the sovereign Lord, "Rather, am I not pleased when they turn from their ways and live?" But if a righteous man turns from his righteousness and commits sin and does the same detestable things the wicked man does, will he live? None of the righteous things he has done will be remembered. Because of the unfaithfulness he is guilty of and because of the sins he has committed, he will die.

—Ezekiel 18:21-24

It seems to me that people want to play with God. They convince themselves that they can live in rebellion and disobedience toward God, ignoring his word and still think that they are pleasing to God. They have convinced themselves that they are not really that bad. I have heard so many times the great lie and excuse, "God knows my heart." To that I have to say, "Indeed he does; he knows your heart is wicked and rebellious." Paul spoke to the Corinthians regarding this, "Do you not know that the wicked will not inherit the kingdom of God? Do not be deceived: Neither the sexually immoral nor idolaters nor adulterers nor male prostitutes nor homosexual offenders nor thieves nor the greedy nor drunkards, nor slanderers nor swindlers will inherit the kingdom of God" (1 Corin. 6:9-10). There are many examples in the Bible regarding who

24

will not make it into the Kingdom of God due to sin. If one also draws back and begins to sin they will also lose that which they once had.

It is no joke to play with sin. We must completely get rid of it from our lives. We may need to spend some time on our knees in prayer repenting and turning from sin. We may need to end relationships, turn from worldly activities, stop going to the movies, and turn off the TV or computer. If you love Jesus you won't desire corruptible things. We may need to seek God to make some serious changes in our lives. We may need to surrender ourselves afresh to the Lord and have him cleanse us. Some of you honestly may never have had a born-again experience and simply need to be saved and filled with the Holy Spirit. Some of you think that you're okay because you attend "church" and are a good person according to your and the

world's standards. But the question is do you have the

witness of the Holy Spirit within you? Can you tell me

when and where you were when Jesus filled you with

his Spirit? Not an emotional experience but one that

completely changed your life, an experience that

caused a fire to become ignited within you for the Son

of God. If you have not had this transformation then it

is time to call on God, repent, seek him, pray, and tarry

for the Holy Spirit. Go back to the old-fashioned ways

of seeking God, repenting, and laying down your life.

It is time to repent, turn from sin, wickedness, stop

pretending like you have it together, humble yourself,

and allow God to change you and truly bless you.

Don't think your sin won't find you out. Don't think

one day you won't stand before God and have to give

an account for your life. Don't let another day go by with an unrepentant heart. Call on Jesus and be willing to forsake sin.

DELIVERANCE

And you will know the truth and the truth will set you free.

—John 8:32

Oftentimes people are in need of deliverance and begin to seek for it. They usually think to go to a deliverance service and get deliverance there. I see three ways people receive deliverance. One would be upon receiving Jesus Christ as their savior. He often gives instant deliverance from things like: drugs, alcohol, fornication, stealing, lying, and sexual immorality, the things that will directly hinder your relationship with him.

Then there are times when after you've been saved, somehow a door to sin is opened or never closed and you may need other Christians or even yourself to lay hands on you and cast the demon or unclean spirit out. To maintain your deliverance, you cannot go back and continue that which you were delivered from or you will again face bondage. The other way one can receive deliverance is by simply obeying God's word.

At one point in my life I was having a hard time with responding when provoked or when things made me angry. I knew my response was not pleasing to God. I would react in anger only to feel ashamed of myself afterwards. At the time another Christian simply told me I needed to obey God, meaning not to return evil for evil and allow the anger to control me, but rather through the spirit exercise self-control. This seemed to be a difficult task for me because not only did I feel I was being mistreated, I didn't know what to do with my emotions. You see, I thought I just needed "deliverance" from anger. I didn't want to go through the pain of the injustice and the hurt I was feeling. However, gradually after practice, obedience, prayer, and reading what God expected from me, I was able to obtain the deliverance through obedience to God's word. The situation did not change, but my response did which gave me peace and victory.

Many times we expect God to just supernaturally deal with the situations in our lives when we are honestly not obeying him. We have to fall out of agreement with our emotions, reactions, and desires to prove ourselves right and simply yield ourselves to God's word. I began to not respond in a negative way, but I kept quiet; this was hard at first, then it got easier. But I still had harsh feelings inside. I didn't want those either so I began to ask God to help me get rid of my internal conflict. And praise God, he even dealt with that.

This is not a one-time quick fix lesson; it has to be practiced day by day. At times I have to "change the channel" in my mind when I hear myself murmuring against what feels like an injustice against me. However, I have the choice to continue on the same channel in my mind or let it go, and change the channel. Again, it's a choice to obey God's word. This is oftentimes a hindrance in deliverance, when people refuse to obey. Deliverance also requires denying yourself, taking up your cross, and following Christ. When Jesus was falsely accused and mistreated, he prayed for his enemies. He did not argue with them; he submitted himself to God. Submitting to God and obeying him is a daily choice and that choice is what will keep us free and walking in our deliverance.

THE CROSS

Weeping may endure for a night but joy comes in the morning.

—Psalms 30:5

I have been crucified with Christ and I no longer live but Christ lives within me. The life I live in the body, I live by faith in the Son of God, who loved me and gave himself for me.

—Galatians 2:20

I do not believe we can experience the cross without pain. The cross' purpose is to kill our "self" life; not alter it, negotiate with it, not compromise with it, but annihilate it completely. This never seems to be an easy task. Remember Jesus on the night he was to face the cross, he went into the garden and prayed and said his "soul was overwhelmed with sorrow to the point of death" (Matt. 26:38). Jesus even asked if it were possible that this cup be taken from him. Meaning as a man he did not want to face what he was about to face, yet in his love and humility he says, "Not my will, but your will be done, Oh, Lord." Jesus was willing to lay down his life that the will of God could be manifested; he never sought after personal gain or ambition. He was willing to endure hardship because he trusted that in doing so his Father would be

36

pleased with him. We too are called to this very mission, maybe not an actual cross made of wood, but one custom made for each one of us. A cross is that which is full of our personal difficulties, trials, pain and suffering. We will face situations far beyond our ability and we will need to fall on our faces and cry out, "Not my will but your will be done." This being the surrendering of our will in exchange for God's will.

My personal experience and the experience of others have taught me this is never an easy path to walk. I know oftentimes this is the turning point for most Christians where they either submit to the will of God or turn back because of the pain and demands to give up their life. They fail to realize this is the path for all that will follow Jesus; however, it is not a doom and gloom life. Like the scripture states, weeping will not last always; it is just the doorway to knowing Jesus, like the cross is the doorway to the resurrection, to life. Before we can have life we must first submit to death. A death to ourselves, though it may not always seem to be for our benefit, we have to know and trust that God knows what is best for us and be willing to embrace the cross he lays before us. I believe that until we have made this a way of life we will not be satisfied.

Sometimes we look back at our lives and tend to see the trials, the hardships, the hurt and the pain. We look at how things seemed to be challenging and focus on our lack. But perhaps had your life been smooth without challenges and hardships and had we received everything we thought we wanted perhaps it would have ruined us. A diamond does not come to its full splendor while still in the earth. No first it is cut from the earth then put in the masters hands and put to the grind. The diamond under goes harsh treatment and much pressure before the Master is finished with it. Only once the master is satisfied will he take the rock from the grind and in his good pleasure will he then be pleased with his work.

The cross is sorely neglected in mans religion "Christendom", which is full of luxuries and ease. The prosperity gospel will not submit to this way of life because it is not easy on the flesh nor does it promote the concept that God will only give us pleasure and prosperity. The cross will put all that to death, all the world has to offer and its cheap thrills. The cross will put to death all of our own agendas and selfish ways. The cross will end all relationships that are not good for us. It will separate us from the world and cause us to have a kingdom mindset. One that says, "I have been crucified with Christ and I no longer live but Christ lives within me. The life I live in the body, I live by faith in the Son of God, who loved me and gave himself for me" (Gal. 2:20). Neither is this an easy path nor is it the wide path, but it is the narrow path and this is why not many are found on it. However to forfeit the path will be an everlasting mistake. Why live for earthly pleasures when this life is but fleeting? Why should we not rather willingly give Jesus our all?

KEEP YOUR EYE ON THE PRIZE

My brethren, I do not consider that I have reached the goal; but this one thing I do know, forgetting those things which are behind, I strive for those things which are before me; I press toward the goal to receive the prize of victory of God's highest calling through Jesus Christ.

—Philippians 3:13-14

When the storms rage and distraction is at every corner, when the trials seem beyond what we can bear, let us remind ourselves to keep our eyes on Jesus. If we give attention to the problems or the enemy or even to our own flesh, they will surely grow and increase. If we forget these distractions and concern ourselves only with our Father, soon the weight of the problem or trial will begin to lose its strength. What we feed will grow. So let us feed the spirit and not the things of the flesh or the situations that go on around us. God is aware of the situation and if we press toward the goal, and that goal is Christ, then we will attain Christ. But if we get off track due to the concerns of this world, we will find ourselves all tripped up over things we cannot control. How much more restful would our walk be with the Lord if we forget the things behind and keep our minds on Christ?

The Bible tells us that "the worries of life and the deceitfulness of wealth" (Matt. 13:22) can choke out the seed of God and make us to be unfruitful. I think it is interesting that in this scripture Matthew mentions the deceitfulness of wealth as well because that can easily become a distraction that draws us away from our goal and one that is commonly justified. God knows all that we are in need of and he will supply for us. The worries of this life can consist of many things: paying bills, relationships, getting through school, starting a business, your future, etc. But when we begin to focus on the goal which should be Jesus, he will lead us to where he wants us to go. Just like a good father will lead his children down the right path in every area of their lives, how much more will our

Heavenly Father lead us to good things?

WE LIVE BY FAITH NOT EMOTION

For his soul does not delight in iniquity, but the righteous man shall live by faith.

—Habakkuk 2:4

How many times have you heard yourself or others say "I feel so…?" I believe we are addicted to how we feel. Our emotions and our feelings can rule us if we neglect to rule them. We want to be moved or feel God's presence. But what if he doesn't show up that way? Do we give up, give in, and think he is not there? What if he wants our devotion despite if we feel him or not.

I have gone through times when in prayer, Bible study, and just day to day life it seemed as if God was nowhere to be found. It usually sort of bothers me, but after having gone through it enough times, I realize that maybe God wants my devotion even if it doesn't stimulate my emotions. Will we still praise him in dry times? Will we still pray and seek him if he doesn't stimulate our emotions? You see, he is worthy to be

46

praised even if he never stimulates our emotions. If we live by how we feel then it is not by faith. We have to have faith that God is there and that he still hears our prayers even if we do not experience him in our emotions.

Our emotions can also be a distraction; sometimes we get all excited over an issue and allow our emotions to be our guide. This can be a dangerous path if our emotions are not in agreement with God's word. I've heard it said, "I just feel this is from God" and the feelings were never gauged by God's word. Feelings can deceive us. Simply think of a time when someone made you mad; you can almost instantly feel your emotions rise up in defense. The Bible tells us we are to be self-controlled. This includes our emotions.

We live in a world that works on our emotions, TV ads, entertainment, books, sales pitches, images of a great life full of luxuries, love stories and songs, and tempestuous images flash before our faces pointing us do whatever feels good and makes us happy or gives us pleasure. This is far from a life in which Jesus calls you to "deny yourself" and does not fit in with the world's promotion of do whatever feels good.

Marriages are ended due to negative emotions, prayers are not petitioned up due to a dry spell in our lives, lives are lost due to an outburst of uncontrollable emotions, relationships are started due to an overload of emotions not in alignment with God's word. Children are conceived out of wedlock due to unchecked emotions running wild. Harmful words and

48

actions come about due to negative emotions. We get an urge and move too fast only later to regret the time and money lost due to a surge of emotions without being prayerful on matters.

Sometimes we have to walk through a lonely and harsh season by faith in spite of how we feel or how our emotions rise up in protest because they are being forced to wait. But it is by Faith that we have to walk out this journey in order for us to reach our destination. A destination perfectly set in the will of God by his hand and at his command and in his time. We should pray that God gives us the power to overcome even the strongest of emotions as we surrender more and more to him.

Some people have been ruled so much by their emotions that I would venture even to say that they have emotional problems. When our emotions are based off of carnal, selfish desires, we move away from God and this can cause a Christian to backslide and the enemy will gladly step in and begin to manipulate a person's emotional health and will take them as far as he can. I believe this plays a big part in why we see so many people suffering from emotional problems like anxiety or depression. They have become obsessed with their own feelings to the point that they have blocked God out. But even this can be healed if we yield our emotions to God's word and begin to obey him and respond to him rather than how we feel.

LOVE

Love is long-suffering and kind, love does not envy; love does not make a vain display of itself and does not boast, does not behave itself unseemly, seeks not its own, is not easily provoked, thinks no evil; rejoices not over iniquity, but rejoices in the truth; bears all things, believes all things, hopes all things, endures all things. Love never fails.

—1 Corinthians 13:4-8

No one can deny this kind of love must come from God. Only he can produce love like this. This is not the love of a fairytale book or a sensual love song or a movie. It is a love full of self-denial and sacrifice. It is a love that can overcome death and the grave. It is the most powerful thing in the world. It changes a dead, sinful person into a child of the Most High God. Love provides a way when there is no earthly way to be seen. Love does not have to obey the laws of nature; it comes straight from the depths of God Almighty. Love stops the mouth of lions and divides the sea. Love pours down manna when there is no other way to find sustenance. Love calls out to the hardest of hearts and finds a soft and gentle place to transform it into the image of Christ.

Love is long-suffering, because we need for him to suffer long with us. We need him to be kind to us in a world full of strife. We need a God who is willing to not give up on us. We need a God who won't hold our mistakes against us as we often do others. We need this kind of love in order for us to become like him; he is love. It is love that wins; not hate, not revenge, not retaliation, not governmental power or education, but love, sweet and pure love from the Father. It is love that drives away fears. It is love that makes us secure. It is love that will enable us to reach the lost. It was love that reached and still reaches us.

The Bible tells us that love never fails and that love is greater than faith or hope because it was for love that Jesus went to the cross and laid his life down for us. It was for love that he came into the world. It is for love that God desires us to come to him. In love he wants our hearts, not out of obligation or habit, but he wants us to love him as he loves us. What value is love if it is not freely given? Let us love the Lord with all our heart, all of our mind, soul and might. If we do this, how can we go wrong?

HOLINESS

Be Holy because I am holy.

—1 Peter 1:16

No one who lives in him keeps on sinning. No one who continues to sin has either seen him or known him. Dear children, do not let anyone lead you astray. He who does what is right is righteous, just as he is righteous. He who does what is sinful is of the devil, because the devil has been sinning from the beginning. The reason the Son of God appeared was to destroy the devil's work. No one who is born of God will continue to sin, because God's seed remains in him; he cannot go on sinning because he has been born of God. This is how we know who the children of God are and who the children of the devil are; anyone who does not do what is right is not a child of God; nor is anyone who does not love his brother.

—1 John 3:6-10

When we are born of God we undergo a transformation. The Bible tells us that we become new creatures in Christ and that the old man is dead; that is the sinful man. We will no longer desire to continue in sin because we have had a complete change within us. This change is a freedom, freedom from sin and bondage. What we do, where we go, how we think, what we read, who are friends are, so much will change that we will no longer be comfortable in a lifestyle saturated in sin because we have been brought out from among sin and now have the Holy Spirit within us.

Holiness comes from a direct relationship with God who is Holy. It becomes a way of life from the inside out as the old man daily submits to Christ. Many people try and act or pretend to be holy, but the truth will show up in their lives. I have heard it said, "The devil can't live right." Holiness is the opposite of all that is in the world: "lust of the body, the covetousness of the eyes, and the pride of material things" (1 John 2:16). It is in the nature of an unregenerated man to live for himself and to naturally yield to the things of this world, just as a born-again man naturally yields himself to God and the things of the Holy Spirit.

Holiness is not just good behavior according to man's standards. Holiness does not originate from man; it originates from God and is implanted within born-again believers through the Holy Spirit. Sin should be viewed as dead in our lives. When God fills us with the Holy Spirit many of our sinful ways instantly leave our body/spirit due to us becoming a new creature and we may never struggle with them

58

again, nor have the desire for them. If the enemy tries to bring them before our face they no longer have power over us unless we reach out to them. We become free from their hold.

Holiness continues on through our walk with Christ. He continues to clean us up as we go along making us more and more in his image. Not that we return to old ways, but areas within us that still need to be taken to the cross and crucified, like, anger, pride, impatience, self-righteousness, or self-ambition: the things that we don't necessarily see within ourselves until God shines the light on them. And praise God, he doesn't ignore what is hiding in us because through this process we continue to walk and remain in his Holiness. Praise the Lord!

YE MUST BE BORN AGAIN

I tell you the truth. No one can see the kingdom of God unless he is born of water and the Spirit. Flesh gives birth to flesh, but the Spirit gives birth to the spirit.

—John 3:5-6

Born again? So on a certain day at a certain time in life, we all have entered this world; this is the day we were born, this being our natural birth from the flesh, from our mother the seed of our earthly father. According to Jesus there must be another birth, one that enables us to see the kingdom of God. He tells us we must be born again, born of the spirit. This spirit is the Spirit of God. In the Bible we see on the day of Pentecost the men and women in the upper room were filled with the Holy Spirit. Throughout the book of Acts we see where people were filled with the Holy Spirit. It happened on a certain day at a time in their lives. It was the day in which they were born of the Spirit of God.

The Spirit takes over and if permitted, will rule our entire lives. The old spirit dies and is no more, unless a person draws back or backslides. The Bible tells us that when the Holy Spirit comes we shall receive power. The power we receive strengthens us to overcome sin and temptation; it leads us in righteousness and holiness. It teaches us the ways of the kingdom of God. The Holy Spirit is alive and active in our lives everyday. Without it we cannot live right or even know God.

Do not be deceived, many people call themselves Christians yet have never been born again. And according to the Bible they do not belong to God: "And if anyone does not have the Spirit of Christ, he does not belong to Christ" (Rom. 8:9). And if you don't belong to God then who do you belong to? A born-again experience will be a day you will not forget. It is an event not a process. His workings in us will be a daily process. It will completely change your entire life.

When we are born of God our Father, we become his seed and as his seed we should produce qualities like him. Our fruit should be: "love, joy, peace, patience, kindness, goodness, faithfulness, gentleness and self-control" (Gal. 5:22-23). The first step in being born again starts with repentance; we must first turn honestly and sincerely from sin. This is not just an emotional action, it is an issue of and in the heart, where we not only turn from sin but have no desire to return. We will feel our will within becoming ready and willing to embrace change. It also originates from the Father; we cannot even be born again until

64

God performs it in us. Yet if we sincerely ask, we will

receive.

SET MY FACE LIKE FLINT

The Sovereign Lord has opened my ears, and I have not been rebellious; I have not drawn back. I offered my back to those who beat me, my cheeks to those who pulled out my beard; I did not hide my face from mocking and spitting. Because the Sovereign Lord helps me, I will not be disgraced. Therefore have I set my face like flint, and I know I will not be put to shame.

—Isaiah 50:5-7

There are going to be times when the situations around us seem impossible or overwhelming and the enemy will come at us with a full arsenal trying to overtake us. This will certainly test us and cause us to either draw back or stand. It is the standing that gives us victory. It is the times when all looks lost when we determine within ourselves that no matter how the situation looks we are going to dig our heels in and stand our ground. A holy boldness will oftentimes come upon us during these times and we rise to the occasion in the power of the Lord and stand like a mighty mountain as the enemy throws every weapon he can at us. During these times we often feel the Lord fighting our battles and it is a great time of rejoicing, rejoicing when it doesn't make any natural sense. But we know man cannot see the work God is doing in our hearts.

The harder the enemy pushes, the more strength we feel from God. We know we have done all we can, so we stand. We set our faces like flint against all the enemy has for us and we hold fast to victory in Jesus. Oh, how sweet the sound of our King fighting for us is, to be able to offer our backs to those who beat us and not turn away or cower. To lay down our lives and see God work it out. To know that if we stand we will not be ashamed because the Lord has it in his hands. Then as the sea settles we see the hand of God and our enemies humbled and scattered. What a mighty God we serve. What joy and peace there is in obeying God. How could we possibly go wrong when we obey? So today let us set our faces like flint and

offer ourselves up knowing that God almighty is

fighting for us and we will not be put to shame.

FATHER OF LIES

He who is a murderer of men from the very beginning and who never stands by the truth, because there is no truth in him. When he speaks he speaks his own lie, because he is a liar, and the father of lies.

—John 8:44

The Bible tells us the Devil is the father of lies and a murderer from the beginning, and that he cannot tell the truth. Many people go around day after day, and year after year believing a lie the enemy told them. Many relationships are destroyed because of a lie that was accepted as the truth. Plans are aborted and lost due to a lie that was accepted as the truth. Many backslidden Christians do not return to the Lord because they have believed a lie about themselves or a lie about the Lord. People remain in bondage because of lies. Names are slandered, Christian unity is disrupted, and many problems arise all from believing a lie.

A lie is a tricky thing because it often appears to be the truth. Once a lie is accepted it gains strength and becomes a stronghold in a person's life. But the

72

Word of God is the Truth. And God is faithful. We become what we believe; the truth or a lie is what makes us. Much like a lie, once the truth is accepted it strengthens us and causes us to become what God wants us to become. It accomplishes God's will in our lives: "So shall my word be that goes forth out of my mouth; it shall not return to me void, but it shall do what I please and it shall accomplish that for which I sent it" (Isa. 55:11).

Sometimes we have believed lies about ourselves for so long that we have developed deep mental paths we have traveled down for years that will take practice to overcome. We will have to train ourselves to cast out the lies the enemy has told us and we have believed over and over again until we have the victory. We have to replace the lies with God's word. If you have believed yourself to be inferior or of no or little value, you will need to tell yourself, "And the Lord shall make you the head, and not the tail, and you shall be on top only, and you shall not be beneath; if you will hearken to the commandments of the Lord your God which I command you this day, to observe and to do them" (Deut. 28:13).

If you have believed you will fail at living right you will have to fall out of agreement with that lie and believe and declare, "I can do all things through Christ who strengthens me" (Phil. 4:13), or "Being confident of this very thing, that he who has begun the good work among you, the same will continue it until the day of our Lord Jesus Christ" (Phil. 1:6). It may take some time and determination to change deep-rooted lies.

74

We recognize a lie when we know the truth. The world has its own version of what the truth is and if we do not look at the Word of God, we will succumb to the world's perverted version of the truth and this will be our ultimate downfall. God is for us and not against us but we can never take hold of this if we continue to believe lies, which is just what our enemy would like.

HIRELINGS

I am the good shepherd; a good shepherd risks his life for the sake of his sheep. But the hired person who is not the shepherd and who is not the owner of the sheep, when he sees the wolf coming, leaves the sheep and runs away; and the wolf comes and seizes and scatters the sheep. The hired person runs away because he is hired and does not care for the sheep.

—John 10:11-13

One day I thought to myself after having read a book on the persecuted church in China, if preachers in America were to preach God's word with no thought of compensation, how quickly we would see church buildings close up and they would serve God no more. They are hired hands and they care not for the flock; they serve for their own gain and not for love. They treat God as their logo. But God has many who have sold all they have and they serve him for love; these are his servants. The others are serving themselves, the world, and even Satan. I have read stories where villages in China gathered all the money they had to send two Christians to the next village to simply spread the gospel.

Spreading the gospel did not become a job or a profession; it became their life's mission without

78

thought of personal gain, unlike what we see in America. We gloat over the titles, *Pastor*, *Bishop*, *Dr.*, *Prophet*, etc. and we think education trumps the power of the Holy Spirit. We dress ourselves up in costly attire to impress the crowds, yet they are void of power and the anointing. While sold-out Christians around the world often sleep in open fields, in corners of homes on the floor, do not have adequate meals, and often suffer great persecution. They offer up their lives as living sacrifices to God. They ask not for luxuries or comfort, but simply to do God's will.

The thought of charging to preach is a concept far from their minds. If Jesus is to be our example then we need to look to him. And nowhere in the scriptures do I see he asked or required money to preach. Nowhere do I see where he sought to increase his material possessions or to form a business in the name of "God." Freely he received and freely he gave. He was not thinking of himself; he was about his Father's business. Many today are about making Jesus their "business" and we see in America that it pays well.

I believe because Jesus was void of any personal gain or acquiring wealth, he had no ulterior motive. He didn't need anyone's money. He didn't use anyone to gain recognition. He was not after a title or winning a popularity contest. He was not seeking fulfillment in a career. He simply came to do his Father's will. Should we not be about our Father's business as well? Is this not the only way to truly have an anointing and the power of the Holy Spirit? The world can see through false motives and agendas, but when we do things out of Love how can we go wrong?

It is *Love* not success, nor religion, nor members, nor

prosperity, nor titles that changes peoples' lives. We

read that the good Shepherd cares for the sheep and

does not run away when the wolf comes. It is *Love* that

changes our lives. Praise God that we have a good

Shepherd.

GOD IS LIGHT AND IN HIM IS NO DARKNESS

God is light and in him is no darkness at all. If we say that we have fellowship with him and yet live in darkness, we lie and do not follow the truth; but if we live in the light as he is in the light, we have fellowship with one another and the blood of Jesus his Son cleanses us from all sin.

—1 John 1:5-7

Light is more powerful than darkness and love is stronger than death. Love never fails and light pierces darkness and the darkness scatters. Love conquers fear, light illuminates, and darkness hides. God is love and light. We must have God's love alive within us or we will not be able to make it or live a holy life. You see, love is not restrained by man. No one could stop Jesus from going to the cross; he willingly went to the cross in love. He was not afraid to love even when no love was returned. He knew the power of Love and walked in the light. He could see the path.

Love exists in light so there is no fear, no discouragement, no lack, and no weakness. Love loves when rejected. It does not need love given in return in order for it to be given. Love is not based on how others react. Love is free to love no matter if received or rejected. God is not limited nor does he withhold his love if we don't love him back. He loved us when we did not love him. He loved us when we go the wrong way and trespass his commands. He does not withhold his love when we are broken and in trouble and don't know what to do. We do not scare him away with our broken lives or our pain. God does not stop loving the sinner or the backslider when they have gone astray. His love stands strong and firm. His love burns bright in this dark world. It is his love that draws us near to him and as we draw near we are able to see the reality of this darkness in the world and the reality of an Almighty God.

In times of great anguish and pain, he is near. We will not always feel his presence but because he said he would never leave us or forsake us, we can rest assured he is there. To have his love and light working within us we must go through a death. It is one thing to have felt his love which changes our lives and yet another thing for his love to live in us. Carnal love produces carnality and is darkness. Godly love produces God and is light. We are not able to love without God in us. We must have his love because as the scripture states, "In the flesh dwells no good thing" (Rom. 7:18). The flesh refuses to love unless love is returned. The love in the flesh is faithful only when faithfulness is returned. Fleshly love rejects if rejected, abuses if abused, hates if hated, and loves if loved. Fleshly love is no love at all.

I once thought I loved only to see the love I had was no love at all; it was a selfish love given only in hopes to receive love in return. But through experience, pain, and hardship the love of God was illuminated in my heart and I understood what real love was.

Know that if we ask for God's love we will have to love when no love is given, we will have to be faithful when unfaithfulness is before us. We will be asked to love when hated, to be kind when abuse is given. The world cannot know this kind of love; it is offensive to the flesh and does not feel good. But upon experiencing this love, we begin to count up the cost and we begin to gain the benefits of following Christ and no man can see this; it is personal and private, but as we follow this love his light will shine through us and will in turn draw people to Jesus.

ONCE SAVED ALWAYS SAVED: A LIE OF SATAN

But there were also false prophets among the people, just as there will be false teachers among you. They will secretly introduce destructive heresies, even denying the sovereign Lord who brought them – bringing swift destruction on themselves. Man will follow their shameful ways and will bring the way of truth into disrepute. In their greed these teachers will exploit you with stories they have made up. Their condemnation has long been hanging over them, and their destruction has not been sleeping. For if God did not spare the angels when they sinned, but sent them to Hell, putting them into gloomy dungeons to be held for judgment; if he did not spare the ancient world when he brought the flood on its ungodly people...

—2 Peter 2:1-5

Not long after I received the Holy Spirit, I was at a Bible study and the pastor told me that we cannot lose our salvation, that once we get saved we are always saved. A girl next to me asked, "Even if we are knowingly in sin?" He said, "Yes, once saved always saved." At the time I didn't believe what he said but I didn't know enough of the scripture right then to ask him about it. Yet, I still didn't believe him and because I had a real born-again experience, I knew I no longer desired to live in sin.

Years later this same false doctrine came back around, but this time it was presented through someone I loved dearly who had been in a backslidden state for years. This person was very happy to hear that even if they willfully sinned and had not repented, God would still allow them in to Heaven and that God would not

90

send them to Hell. I heard this person tell me this with joy and declare this as divine revelation from God, which gave this person hope.

My heart sank and I asked if what he believed could be backed up by the word of God? He quickly turned on me and began to tell me the revelation must not be for me, and that I couldn't understand it because I wasn't seeing it in the Spirit. I responded that it wasn't for me, then I asked him how he would get past the scripture: "The wages of sin is death" (Rom. 6:23) and the scripture, "He didn't spare the angels who had sinned" (2 Peter 2:4). This led me to search the scriptures for myself on this matter. Many scriptures came to my mind and I presented a few to him. He simply found an excuse to discredit them all and he simply said I did not understand the scripture.

"But if you do warn the wicked man and he does not turn from his wickedness or from his evil ways, he will die for his sin" (Ezek. 3:19). "Once saved always saved" is a false doctrine presented by false teachers and treats the blood of Jesus with contempt. Even a child knows that when they do wrong there are consequences, but the rebellious want to find a way to justify their rebellion against God. The Bible tells us that "men loved darkness rather than light because their deeds were evil" (John 3:19).

When we live by the Spirit there is no way we can comfortably continue in sin. We will suffer in ourselves by the chastisement of the Holy Spirit when we err. We will be most miserable, but if we continue to ignore the Spirit we will find ourselves on the road to destruction and Hell. Once saved always saved is a lie from the enemy and believed by the rebellious.

Read 2 Peter 2 and study to show yourself approved.

GOD DOES NOT MAKE COOKIE–CUTTER PEOPLE

For you created my inmost being; you knit me together in my mother's womb. I praise you because I am fearfully and wonderfully made; your works are wonderful, I know that full well. My frame was not hidden from you when I was made in the secret place. When I was woven together in the depths of the earth, your eyes saw my unformed body. All the days ordained for me were written in your book before one of them came to be.

—Psalm 139:13-16

When my son was in about the third grade, I began to see him coming home acting, speaking, and singing in a certain way imitating the other kids at school because I knew those ways were not from him. This bothered me and I would say to him, "Who are you today? That's not you. Just be yourself. I like who God made you." Then one night I was at a school function with him and the Lord began to show me some things. I saw this couple in front of me and then another couple came in and sat next to them and you could tell they knew each other. As I looked at them, they seemed to all be dressed alike, their hair styles were alike, and they seemed very similar and God said, "I don't make cookie-cutter people. I made every person unique."

I then thought about my own life and how so

many times I tried to be someone I was not in order to be accepted or loved. I tried to be the woman I thought my husband wanted in order to receive his love. I tried to look a certain way to fit in or so people would like me. I tried to make a good impression on others in order to win their affection or favor. But God let me know that this is nothing more than trying to manipulate people into liking and accepting me and that is not being honest or real. He said people lose their whole identity trying to be something they are not.

I thought about my son. And I told him I want him to grow and become what God has designed him to be, not the standards set by men or what man has forced upon him. I believe it has taken God years to even begin to unwind the entangled lies I have become because of my years of trying to win the love of man. It has taken the Love of God to even reveal this to me. I could not see it within myself. But praise God, he is faithful and he has begun to shine the light on this area in my life that I might be set free.

When we dare to be ourselves and who God made us to be, know that the enemy will reject us. He wants us to imitate him and he too wants people created in his image. God makes us free to be ourselves, just as he has designed us to be. If God made your hair curly, it pleased God for you to be that way. If God made you tall, it pleased God for you to be that way. If you have a dry sense of humor, it pleased God for you to be that way. If God made you a serious person, it pleased God for you to be that way. He made you and he was pleased with what he made. If you hate how you look, then you have believed the lies of Satan who has told you that what God made was not good enough.

God made us and he chose our personality, appearance, talents, gifts, likes, and dislikes. Some people like the walls in their home painted green, some like yellow. Be just who God made you to be and you can't go wrong; people will always like and dislike you but remember God was pleased with what he made. God will never call you ugly, or less than, but he will call you his own. He will say I have wonderfully and fearfully made you. Remember after God made man he looked and saw that it was good. He calls us the "apple of his eye" (Psa. 17:8).

WAITING FOR ISAAC AND FORSAKING ISHMAEL

Get rid of the slave woman and her son, for that slave woman's son will never share in the inheritance with my son Isaac.

—Genesis 21:10

When the Lord makes a promise to us it doesn't always show up instantly; it sometimes requires faith and patience to obtain it. Remember Abraham's promise of a son to be born. Sarah grew impatient for the promise and took Hagar her handmaid and gave her to Abraham to try and bring forth the promise. They took matters into their own hands and a child was born, Ishmael, but not the one that was promised. Ishmael teased and mocked his brother Isaac after he was born. In the heart of Ishmael was resentment because even he knew he was not the chosen one. Isaac was the promise and because of Sarah's disobedience, they suffered the rebellion of Ishmael and even to this day the world suffers. Isaac was God's choice and not Ishmael. Yet so often we chose our own efforts over God's choice and we suffer from the works of our disobedience and impatience.

Waiting for God's promises to come to pass can cause much discomfort. The marriage seems over while God calls you to wait on him until he fixes it; all the while voices around you are telling you to divorce. And what about the minister who eagerly waits for the right time to go forth with God's word as they watch others go about as they please. Consider the saint who sits alone in a jail cell because of persecution is stirring in their bones like fire and the call of God is on their life, but it all seems dead and wasted.

The promise is sure, but the time is unknown. The date of its arrival is not given and may even seem as dead as Sarah's womb was. When we have exhausted all of our own efforts we come to the place of nothing, to the place of abandonment and surrender.

When it is no longer we who live but Christ has come alive in us. Then late, perhaps in the midnight hour, our Lord walks in and hand-delivers the promise.

I wonder how many have abandoned the wait and settled for Ishmael. How many have refused to wait for God's promises and taken hold of their own understanding and now suffer because they have not been willing to suffer the shame and bear the burden that comes with following and waiting on God. How many have said, "No" to God and his plan and allowed the enemy to come into their camp and steal from them because they gave up and refused to wait on Jesus' hand-delivery. If he has promised it, your mind should be made up and you should be willing to wait no matter how long. Your heart should be compelled to follow after him who promised it. What other choice do you really have?

If we are not for Christ then we are against him. If we are not obedient to Christ we are disobedient and rebellious to him who knows what is best for us. What a tragedy it is when we think we know what is best for our own lives. If this is where you are then there is hope, but it starts with surrender and acceptance of what God has for you. And it takes courage and determination to wait on God. We often want what is easiest and comfortable, but it gets us nowhere and only causes problems. Jesus could have chosen to live a life of luxury but he knew what he was after could only be found in the cross. And we too can only find what we are looking for at the cross. Take your time and expectation to the cross and go to Jesus; he will give you what he promised when the time is right according to God's will.

Remember also that which is not from God will harass and try to take what God has ordained, just as Ishmael wanted what could only be given to Isaac because it was appointed by God. If Ishmael had stayed with Abraham in Isaac's presence, I believe there would have been years of strife and conflict between the children and that could have caused more problems. This is why we have to forsake Ishmael and our own efforts and rely on God to bring the promise to pass.

VIRTUE

Whoever walks in integrity walks securely, but he who makes his ways crooked will be found out.

—**Proverbs 10:9**

Virtue: conformity to the standard of right; behavior showing high moral standards; morally good behavior or character.

—**Merriam-Webster Dictionary**

I once overheard a conversation and the talk of seeing someone naked was brought up. A child was listening and innocently said, "Oh, yuck, who would want to see her naked?" But the other people began to say, "Oh wait till you're a little older you'll think differently." This didn't set right with me then later the Lord began to talk to me about virtue. He said the world thinks it is normal for a young person that comes of age to begin to lust, first with their eyes then with their actions. They say what is wrong is right and what is right is wrong.

Virtue is not honored or in style for the world. The conversation was a way of thinking that was not in agreement with God's word. I know that people, young or old can live a life of virtue and integrity and in agreement with God's word. If a child is taught that it

108

is wrong to lust with their eyes and to chase after the things of this world, then when he or she comes of age and has received God's word as their own truth, he or she will not desire to go down that path, unless they have fallen out of agreement with God's word, or if they do not have the Holy Spirit.

People often base their morals on what is acceptable to the world's standard and not according to God's word. They judge according to the choices they have made and justify themselves and excuse others and fail to keep a Godly standard. They look at one another and judge standards of conduct according to what they see and from what I see that is a grievous choice. We are bombarded with sexual images all over the place, at the stores, on TV, and the Internet. Just look out your door and I am sure it won't take long to see a man or woman dressed to seduce, music to persuade, and actions to demoralize all of mankind. We live in perilous times, not only for our young people but also for our families.

We see corruption in places it ought not to be and it is merely overlooked so no one is offended, and it is even accepted as the normal. No one stands up in outrage when sin is running rampant in the church, the body of Christ. They do not "expel the immoral brother" (1 Corin. 5:13), rather they chose to sit up in the mess and expect not to get corrupted by it. That's like expecting a child to sit in a mud puddle and not get dirty. "A little leaven leavens the whole lump" (Gal. 5:9).

They begin to look at one another and base

110

their morals and virtue on what they see and not on God's Holy word. How many times have we heard of "leaders" who have fallen while it was known that they were engaging in sin and nothing was said or done, then the fellowship soon begins to deteriorate from a lack of virtue and Holiness? Then in time God exposes it and they all hang their heads. Even then, often times their remorse is merely due to getting exposed, not because they have Godly sorrow. They often just brush their sin under the rug as if it is no big deal and soon they return to leadership, unrepentant and full of sin. If we walk uprightly according to God's word we do not have to fear being exposed. If we live a transparent life we are honest with God and man and we do not have to hide, this is the freedom of a life lived with virtue.

112

I AM NOT A TYRANT

I have loved you with an everlasting love; I have drawn you with loving kindness.

—Jeremiah 31:3

<u>Tyrant</u>: an absolute ruler unrestrained by law or constitution. A usurper of sovereignty; a ruler who exercises absolute power oppressively or brutally; one resembling an oppressive ruler in the harsh use of authority or power.

—Merriam-Webster Dictionary

A tyrant is one who demands your obedience for his selfish gain. A tyrant does not want obedience because he loves you, rather he does not love at all. He uses you to get what he wants, then when he is done with you he will begin to mistreat you, abandon, or try to annihilate you all together because you are no longer of any value to him. He will abuse you and try to establish fear in you to control you for his own profit and will. A tyrant is never satisfied and never pleased. He demands and demands and offers only enough to you to keep you going for his greed; when his lust is satisfied, you are no longer of any good to him. He will praise you only when you have fulfilled his desires and reject you when you no longer are submitted to him in obedience. A tyrant will ask you to give all for him and promise you lies or take your freedom all

114

together. He will demand and use force to get his way.

God is not a tyrant, nor will he compromise with man. In God's loving kindness he draws us near. If we refuse to live our lives according to his will, which is best for us and holds eternal life, He simply lets us go our own way. He will not force us, mistreat and threaten us, or abuse us to conform to his will. In love He will reach out to us for our own good. He will not force any one to serve him either; one serves God because he wants to.

The conflict between our will and God's will rests only on the side of our unsurrendered life. Once we have surrendered we have peace, fellowship, and unity with Jesus. He does not want anyone to serve him out of obligation but rather out of Love. Jesus did not die for us out of obligation but out of his great Love for the Father and for us. No spouse wants their mate to spend time with them out of obligation but rather out of love. You see, God is an all or nothing God. He wants it all or you can go your own way. No spouse wants a half-committed wife or husband. God doesn't want us to be half-committed to him. In order for a marriage to work it must be an all or nothing commitment. A half-faithful spouse doesn't make for a very good relationship nor does it with our Lord.

He will not compromise with us in order to make us comfortable. He knows what is best and he does not want harm to come to us. No more would a parent compromise with their child and allow them to play with fire just because they cry and want to; the parent knows the danger that could befall the child and is unwilling to compromise with that child's will. How much more does our Lord Jesus Christ want to keep us out of the fires of Hell? We can trust him even when we don't understand what is going on. Sometimes we are like the young child that is unable to see the dangers that could befall when unsupervised.

We have a Heavenly Supervisor with eternal rewards in His hand. Will you trust him with your life? Will you walk with him even when all seems unclear and unsure? Will you trust him with childlike trust because he loves us for our own good, both now and for eternity? "O how narrow is the door and how difficult is the road which leads to life, and few are those who are found on it" (Matt. 7:14). "And a highway shall be there, and it shall be called the way of holiness; the unclean shall not pass over it; and there

117

shall be no road beside it; fools shall not err therein"

(Isa.35:8).

LILY OF THE VALLEY

I am a rose of Sharon, a lily of the valleys. Like a lily among thorns is my darling among the maidens.

—Song of Solomon 2:1-2

Often time we start out on a path thinking of the bright future with hope and determination in our hearts, eyes steady ahead. When we first start we joyfully tend to the task at hand; not concerned with the toil, not aware of any strain. We are content and happy on the path. We expect the smoothness to continue on until we reach our final goal but soon the road takes a turn and our bright future now appears bleak, our hopes turn to discouragement, and our joy turns to toil. We face hardships and adversity we could have never imagined while the path was smooth and easy. Yet in our low state we keep pressing on, hoping this too shall pass.

And indeed it does pass and our future once again looks hopeful. We pass through the same low valley a few times and always manage to make it through. We begin to see the valley as merely a stepping stone along the way. So we continue on our way hopeful of the future. Another valley appears and we brace ourselves for the toil, but this time the valley is exceedingly deep and storm clouds begin to form; yet we find the courage to press on. We press on but this time there seems to be no bottom to the depths of the valley and the dark clouds have turned into a downpour. Going on is merely impossible and turning back seems to be a letdown after having come so far.

The future has now been lost in the toil of each step and the mental anguish calls for us to simply give up. We cannot see beyond the valley's depth or the raging storm. Our spirit is weak within us to the point of giving up. And now to make matters worse, everyone who once traveled with us has determined to turn back and ridicule our convictions. We are now alone without hope, courage, and without companionship.

Our dilemma is do we too turn back or do we yet wait to see if the storm will pass and if the vision of the future will be restored? Will we again find hope and courage or would it be all together better to give up and turn back? So for days and weeks we remain unmoved waiting to know what to do. The wait yet adds another burden to our already strained mental state. In a way we feel as if we have already given up. We feel like we are just wishing and hoping for it all to fall apart so we can say, "See. I knew it would never work."

We feel paralyzed by the dilemma, and we barely notice the rain has begun to lighten and the sky has begun to break and the sun has begun to shine. All we can see is the future through deep, valley eyes. Our courage is gone and we never again want to face this valley. It has taken all of our life and strength. The future seems to be a burden and we can't seem to get a solid hold.

We are still alone so we have no one to confide in, just the deep valley. At this we notice the sun is shining and the day is new, but we cannot see through the valley to the other side. We decide to get up and just simply walk in the sunlight down into the depths of the valley. Our heart is scared and our hope is nearly gone but the day is pleasant so we try to take it in. We soon begin to find treasures in the valley we had never noticed before: berries and fruits, winding streams, and beautiful flowers along the valley's path. Soon our minds are at ease as our eyes begin to take in the splendor of the deep valley. Its aroma is sweet and pleasant. We no longer feel the loneliness of having no companions. We sense a peace and a joy and it has seemed to have replaced all of our toil and discouragement.

I see the most beautiful lilies along the path that seem to be encouraging me on. I stop to admire one and as I am standing there I recall the journey I have been on and that I started so long ago. I can see that though it all I was never really alone and I begin to sense that if the path had always remained on the high ground and I had never had to travel into the valley alone, I would have never made it to where I am today,

124

in the splendor of the valley. I am reminded of the rose of Sharon, of the Lily of the Valley. "Like a lily among thorns is my darling among the maidens. Like an apple tree among the trees of the forest is my lover among the young men. I delight to sit in his shade and his fruit is sweet to my taste. He has taken me to the banquet hall. And his banner over me is love" (Song of Sol. 2:1-4). The banner of love that is over me was withheld from my eyes until I made it to the depths of the valley, where I find comfort in the Lily of the Valley, the Rose of Sharon.

FAITH, FEAR AND MAN

Now faith is the substance of things hoped for, as it was the substance of things which have come to pass, and it is the evidence of things not seen.

—Hebrews 11:1

For it is through faith we understand that the worlds were framed by the word of God, so that the things which are seen came to be from those which are not seen.

—Hebrews 11:3

I can do all things through Christ Jesus who strengthens me.

—Philippians 4:13

A world driven by fear says don't even try it. Don't get your hopes up. Don't count your chickens before they hatch. The statics are not in your favor. It is too hard. Many times these are the words not only from without but also from within.

When God began to think about creating the earth and man, if man had been there to consult with God, I am sure man would have tried to discourage him with words like, "Oh God, how can you do that? Are you saying you're going to make something out of nothing? Impossible!" "The statistics are not in your favor, God!" "That is crazy." "You're going to make what, an earth and a man out of what?" I am sure the critics would have waged war against God's idea of creation.

"The earth was without form and void; and darkness was upon the face of the deep. And the spirit of God moved upon the face of the water. And God said, 'Let there be light, and there was light'" (Gen. 1:1-3). "I believe, therefore have I spoken" (Ps. 116:10). "Death and life are in the power of the tongue; and those who love it shall eat the fruits there of" (Prov. 18:21). There is power in the spoken word. As God began to think of the earth and man, they became dear to his heart. So he simply spoke his desires into existence and saw that it was good. "And God saw that the light was good" (Gen. 1:3). He saw that the earth was good, that man was good; all he created was good and he blessed it.

A man named Nehemiah was commissioned to rebuild Jerusalem after it had been destroyed and had

129

been in ruins for years. He obeyed the command of God. As he worked on rebuilding, an army was sent to daily mock and ridicule his efforts and his dream, a dream birthed within him from God. Nehemiah found strength in God and turned his face against the opposition and finished his task of rebuilding Jerusalem. He kept the vision before him and did not shrink back in the face of adversity.

David faces Goliath, a man twice, maybe three times David's size. Goliath was a man of war versus a young shepherd boy. David was not intimated by Goliath's size, words, or reputation. David knew God was with him and that God would fight his battles. David believed and found victory that day, and a giant was slain by a young, inexperienced boy. Nothing is too hard for God. No mountain too high. No dream too big. No valley too deep, especially when the dream in from God.

"There is no fear in love, but perfect love casts out fear, because fear is torment. He who fears is not made perfect in love" (1 John 1:18). "For you have not received the spirit of bondage, to be in fear again" (Rom. 8:15). "I shall not fear what man shall do unto me" (Heb. 13:6). In a world in bondage to fear, how does a man overcome and achieve his dreams and still have peace with God? Not by way of the world's standards, that only leads man into more bondage and continual striving. The answer is so simple that many reject it. The answer is also not dependent upon man, so therefore many reject it.

Faith will build great cities and make great men. Fear will tear them down and step on their ruins. Faith says, "I can." Fear says, "I cannot." Faith says, "I have." Fear says, "I have not." Faith builds you up and encourages your soul. Fear destroys and buries your life. Faith takes courage. Fear just simply gives up or never tries. A man without God unknowingly destroys his own life. A man with God achieves great things and finds rest for his soul in peace, in love, in faith, in hope, and in knowing that he is pleasing to his maker.

THEY PREACH ANOTHER JESUS

I wish you to be patient with me for a while, so that I may speak plainly, and I am sure you will be. For I am zealous for you with the zealousness of God, for I have espoused you to a husband, that I may present you as a pure virgin to Christ. But I am afraid that just as the serpent through his deceitfulness mislead Eve, so your minds should be corrupted from the sincerity that is in Christ. For if he who has come to you preaches another Jesus, whom we have not preached, or if you have received another spirit, which you had not received, or another gospel, which you had not accepted, you might have listened to him.

—2 Corinthians 11:1-4

I have to raise the question, how have we seen Jesus portrayed in America, especially in the last handful of years? What are the images and examples we are given? We turn the TV on and we see hour after hour of preachers fighting for primetime TV slots, gorgeously arrayed in fine clothes proclaiming Jesus will bless you, he will make you rich if you give, think the right thoughts, hold fast to your dreams, etc. We see men and women who portray Jesus as their Lord as they sell tickets to their next big event. We see them indulging in all sorts of luxuries, cruises, extravagant buildings and building projects, grand choirs decked in colorful robes. We have power structures set up in the denominations; hierarchies from smallest to greatest. We see a Jesus of excess and luxury.

Yet my Bible does not portray this kind of

Jesus. The Jesus of the Bible said to the scribe who came to him saying he would follow him in Matthew 8:20, "The foxes have holes, and the birds of the air a resting place, but the Son of man has nowhere even to lay his head." He did not even have a rented home or even an apartment of his own. He tells his disciples when he sent them out to take with them "no money in their purse" Mark 6:8.

I find nowhere in the Bible where Jesus took up an offering or where he paid himself a salary. I find nowhere in the Bible where Jesus charged admission to heal or to hear him preach. He didn't own a jet or a building, or a car or even a donkey. He owned nothing that I can see of any value, some clothes and shoes, that's about it. Does this line up with what we see in man-made religion they call "church?"

I do not find in the Bible where he organized a group of people and dressed them in fancy robes and sang to entertain the crowds. I see nowhere in the Bible where Jesus encouraged people to acquire great wealth and live in luxury and ease. He told the rich man to sell all that he had and then come and follow him. This does not mean that it is a sin to have things, but I encourage you to look at what you are striving after and for what. God knows what we need and he will provide our every need. But we need to look at the Jesus of the Bible. The Jesus of the Bible was not well-received by the world. The scribes and the Pharisees all disliked and even hated him. I declare to you today that they teach another Jesus. Not the true Jesus; the Jesus they teach is a Superstar Jesus.

Christ went among the people and lived his life.

He did not call the people to meet with him every Sunday at 10:00 a.m. for a service and that he would begin with some songs, then a collection, then a prayer, then preach, then pray again and dismiss everyone to go home and eat chicken. No, this is not the Jesus of the Bible and he never held a rummage sale, a bake sale, a fashion show, a single's meeting; he never renamed a pagan holiday and copied its pagan practices. He never set up a youth group or invented programs and events to bring people to him. He had no marketing team. He never gave an altar call or an invitation to join his "church." No, this is not the Jesus of the Bible. Search the Bible for yourself and see. Seek him out in the pages of the Bible I am sure he will look different than what is presented in the institution every week. He didn't have to offer programs to draw crowds or advertise to gain followers. The people were hungry and he had the food they sought after.

We got the Jesus of the Baptist's, Pentecostals, Apostolic, Lutherans, Non-denominations, etc., and the list goes on. The Bible asks us, was Christ divided? Why are there so many denominations? In the book of Acts they were all on one accord and they were of one mind. Through the years the spirit of division and denomination came in and fragmented and even changed the gospel based on their doctrines, so much so that there is great confusion on the very Word of God. But Jesus never changes so therefore we must look at ourselves and investigate where all this came from and go back to Jesus and his Word.

138

DECEPTION

Then you will know the truth and the truth will set you free.   —**John 8:32**

Deceive: to take, ensnare, to be false to, to fail to fulfill, cheat, to cause to accept as true or valid what is false or invalid, to give a false impression.

True or truth: in accordance with fact or reality, rightly or strictly so called; genuine, real or actual, exactly in tune, correctly positioned or aligned; upright or level, loyal or faithful, accurately conforming to, bring into the exact shape or position required.

If one does not believe the truth, it does not change the fact that it is still true: 1+1=2. This is a fact, yet to the unlearned or ignorant they may debate it or not even know it, yet 1+1=2. Many people hear and know the truth of what Gods word says, yet they deny that it applies to them or they say that is just what *you* believe. Even when what you believe is really not yours, it is God's word.

Our enemy who is called a deceiver and the father of lies has deceived the nations. He has deceived many into believing a lie. They may have heard the truth of God's word yet the enemy has come in through sin and gotten them to believe that they do not need to believe God's word. Often times when one presents the truth, they are looked upon as a liar or as a deceiver. They said that Jesus deceived the people, that
140

he had a devil, that he was crazy. Yet in him is the truth and no lie.

When one is deceived, they themselves do not usually know it. Maybe they have a feeling that something is wrong yet they cannot put their finger on it. Through deception they become slaves to that which they serve. You cannot serve two masters; whoever commits sin is a servant of sin. Deception is a powerful tool of the enemy; yet deception is not a new trick.

Remember Eve in the garden; she was the first woman who believed a lie and was deceived. The enemy tempted her and she succumbed. His tricks are not greater today than they were then and man is no further from the same position today that Eve was back then. The enemy will always try to appeal to our flesh and demand obedience to him and disobedience to God. Here is the trick; disobedience to God only brings bondage and more deception. The blinders become thicker and visibility becomes low, perhaps even developing total blindness.

We all have been deceived and walked in deception, but God is not afraid of the enemy's tricks. God does not play games; He is all-powerful. He does not need tricks. If you have come into the knowledge of Jesus and he has shed his grace on you and you are knowingly still in sin and still feel unwilling to let it go, but you are grieved by the Holy Spirit over this matter, there is hope for you.

God is faithful. There have been times in my life when the Lord has brought certain issues up to my attention and I've said, "Lord I'm not ready for this." One time someone had done something wrong against me and hurt me terribly; my heart ached for a long time over this thing. And I was angry on the inside and I felt justified in this because that person had wronged me. Well, God brought this up to me and I said, "No" to him for a while, but you see God does not give up on us, nor will he change his mind.

The torment of disobeying God was worse than my anger and hurt feelings. I just went before God and said, "Lord, I know this anger is wrong inside me and I want you to change that person, but I want your will in my life. I know I'm wrong and that my heart is wrong. Please, Lord, I want my heart to be right." I then had to begin to cleave to God's word, casting out the

anger, refusing to think on how I'd been mistreated. I had to begin to see that person in God's love and to get my mind off of me and past events.

God gave me the strength to do this and he then opened my eyes to see how the person who hurt me was in terrible bondage and it wasn't that person who was trying to hurt me, but the enemy using that person. The Lord began to have me start praying for that person instead of being angry. I began to be able to love rather than hate. This cannot be obtained while we still hold on to sin. We must denounce it, turn from it, and obey God's word.

CHRISTIANS WITHOUT CHRIST

For not all who are descended from Israel are Israel. Nor because they are his descendants are they all Abraham's children. On the contrary, "It is through Isaac that your offspring will be reckoned." In other words, it is not the natural children who are God's children, but it is the children of the promise who are regarded as Abraham's offspring.

—Romans 9:6-8

Have you ever met a person who goes on and on telling stories about who they are and all that they have? Stories told to impress the listener, some so exaggerated and extravagant all who hear know they are listening to a liar. It is often stories of great possessions when the person they are bragging to knows good and well he or she does not have what he or she claims to have. Some may not be so extravagant; some simply stretch the truth to make themselves seem more than they really are. No doubt we have all stood in audience to a person like this. What about those who are deceived? They believe they have or are something they really do not have or are not. It's like an alcoholic not thinking he or she has a problem, or an abusive spouse who blames their abuse on the spouse. Or what about the rich, powerful and

146

famous who live a life of luxury, who show forth a lifestyle to be envied by the world, yet day after day they live on drugs and go from one relationship to another, unhappy and in turmoil.

Deception can convince a person that a lie is the truth. Some of the enemy's tricks of deception are subtle and have a thread of the truth running through them, seeming right but truly are false. People equate doing good deeds with being a good, righteous Christian. But what if what is being done is not for Christ but for their self-centeredness, or self-righteous motives? So what makes a person a Christian?

Christians without Christ, you may say how can that be? Christ is the essential of being a Christian. Yes, Christ is essential to being a Christian; however, we live in a world where much is done in the name of

Christ but not done by his will or his plan. In the Old Testament, Isaiah 30:1-2 says, "'Woe to the obstinate children,'" declares the Lord, "'to those who carry out plans that are not mine, forming an alliance, but not by my Spirit, heaping sin upon sin; who go down to Egypt without consulting me; who look for help to Pharaoh's protection, to Egypt's shade for refuge.'" These days much is done in the name of Jesus but not according to his command. We have a nation of people that call themselves Christians, but in their day to day lives there is no Christ. They have become Christian actors on Sunday mornings and are in the company of other Christian actors, but in their homes, at work, in their social lives, and in their relationships, Christ does not exist. We are told you will know a tree by its fruit. What kind of fruit do you bring forth?

THE SEARCH IS OVER

If you confess with your mouth "Jesus is Lord," and believe in your heart that God raised him from the dead, you will be saved. For it is with your heart that you believe and are justified, and it is with your mouth that you confess and are saved.

—Romans 10:9-13

I could do nothing to save myself. I was not even looking for Jesus when he came to me. At least I didn't realize it was Jesus I was looking for. All my life I sought to fill the emptiness that was inside. I went down many avenues in search of wholeness, only to end up even emptier. The hole inside became filled up with sin and pleasures. I loved my sin and thought one day I would find the answer. I could not save myself. Nothing I did filled up the emptiness. Yet I searched for an answer. When the true answer of Christ presented itself, I rejected the idea. I thought if I gave myself to Jesus, it would be an end to my way of life and a road to restriction.

I couldn't deliver myself from the bondage that was in my life; the pain and shame only mounted. I would try to avoid the areas in my life that seemed to

150

cause the most trouble; however, I would go back to the mess, to that which I hated and loved. It was like I was caught in a terrible cycle I couldn't break free from. Everything was a mess, yet I tried to keep myself together. There was no major downfall, no big tragedy, no big problem, just one day he came to me. I began to be terribly disturbed, yet something on the inside of me began to open up. I began to touch and sense a Love so comforting and so final. I knew I was going to go there.

It was Jesus, the Almighty God, my true and only creator coming to me, a defiled and sinful person. I was full of filthiness and shame, yet he came to me; he who is pure, he who has no sin, no filth, no impurities. I tell you I did not know it was He who my soul sought after, not everything I chased and

151

destroyed and defiled myself with. For a few weeks he was heavy upon me and my heart was in a struggle. My life was in the balance. Would he have come to me again? I cannot say. Would any other time have worked? I cannot say. But I became ready. His Love increased and all the things around me I once loved seemed unworthy in comparison to what was taking place on the inside of me. No man could see it; no natural eye could detect it. It was something on the inside of me. It's like a man who searches his whole life for something and finds it. No jewel could compare, like nothing in this world could compare to that which was taking place on the inside of my heart.

So I cried out to God in hope that I would pass over to him. Did I know for sure? No. Did I have anything to hold on to? Not really. Just a few words I had read in the Bible, "If you confess with your mouth and believe in your heart that Jesus Christ is Lord, you shall be saved." I had that and the thing I could never truly describe that was growing on the inside of me. I could not save myself. And why did he choose me? What did he see in me?

What was it, Lord? You knew me before I was formed in the womb and to this day you keep me. You, Oh Lord, are my keeper. No man can say this is his work. No man can boast of his doings. No man has ever touched me like Jesus has. You alone are my life and my love. You alone, oh precious Savior, are my shepherd, my high tower and my refuge.

So if you feel like no one understands and no one knows you, I say to you there is one. I understand being on the edge of life and death. The path you've been on is one you know and the other side is distant and unknown. But He will fill the emptiness inside; He is what and whom you seek after. You're not crazy and you're not so far gone that his hand cannot reach you. He loves you and his mercies are new every day. On the other side is restoration and a restored relationship with the Father. You will face trouble, you will make mistakes, and you will stumble and fall. There will be days when you feel overwhelmed and you wonder if he is there or if he really cares. There will be times of great joy and peace, understanding, and love. But in all these things he will never leave you nor forsake you. And he will cause many trials to come into your life in order that you might learn from him, the way he wants you to.

He sometimes seems to break us up so much that we are unable to turn any way but to him. See, he will receive the glory; we are no longer our own, we are his and he wants us to become one with him. In him is everything we need. In him alone are we to live, breathe, and have our being. When he sees things in us that are not like him, he goes after them, to destroy them. There are things in us only he can see and only he knows how to rid us of. I am telling you no man will ever deal with you like Jesus will. He alone loves you and can restore you. Trust him with your life and you will not be disappointed.

LOVE NEVER FAILS

Love never fails.

—1 Corinthians 13:8

And now these three remain; faith, hope and love. But the greatest of these is love.

—1 Corinthians 13:13

The love of the world continually fails. Most times it is based on what we can get from someone or what they can do for us. It's self-centered love. When things get hard or difficulties come, the love of the world diminishes. Why? Because it is based on self and not true love, the love of God. You see, God so loved the world that he gave his only begotten son. He gave his son to die as a sacrifice in order that you and I may have reconciliation back with the Father and so that we may be able to know the Father. Love in the world is often based on emotions, lust, and selfishness. Observe a child; they hold no resentment, they keep no bitter memories, and they do nothing to avenge themselves or to defend themselves. And surprisingly, the one at the other end seems to find it easy to love such a one. God loves us and we are to love others with his love in return.

So many marriages fail because they are not based on God's love. When times get hard and problems arise they fall apart. They fall apart because of unfulfilled self-centered love. Love of the world and its ways can never satisfy. The enemy is never content and seeks only to kill, steal, and destroy. When we become impatient and bitter toward our spouses, family members, friends and others, we have slipped into selfish love and away from God's love. When our thoughts are always against others, our thoughts are not like God's thoughts. When we so readily give up and refuse to put up with it any more, take heed and know that you have slipped from God's love into selfish, worldly love. When everything others say and do makes us angry, be aware; self-love is rising. Yes, I know there may be situations you face that are beyond your doing and that are very painful to go through, but Jesus is always there to comfort you and he will help you through if you call upon him.

Many times you may realize that you cannot do what is being asked of you, but Jesus has given you his Holy Spirit to you to help you. And one day you will look back and say, "If I did not have the Lord who is on my side, I would have surely perished." You see, He is strong when we are weak. He is lifted up when we are humble before him. Love will prevail but only when all of the selfish love of the world has been taken out of us. Usually this comes by way of fire and affliction. God desires a pure heart and when he sees worldly love in our hearts, he goes after it to purge us

160

of it. Purging comes by way of a cross. When we have died to the love of self then we can love as God loves.

If in our personal relationships we are filled with envy when another is blessed or lifted up in any way, we do not have the love of God. If we secretly rejoice when one fails, or when one is going through hard times, or times of great difficulty, then we do not have the love of God. When we desire to be lifted up above others and admired, it is worldly. If we think evil of others, it is worldly. God is for us and not against us. He looks beyond the seen into the unseen and he requires us to do the same. He does not tell us to put any trust in what is seen; rather he says that we are not to live by sight but by faith.

Yet this faith is nothing if we do not have love in our hearts. The greatest commandment is, "Love the

Lord your God with all your heart, mind and with all your strength and love your neighbor as yourself" (Luke 10:27). Do you desire mercy, patience, understanding, grace, blessing, favor and love? Then these are the things you are to give. "God will judge every man according to their works, only he sees the heart of man" (Rom. 2:6).

The definition of love is not what the world sings about or how the world or TV portrays love. "Love is long-suffering and kind. Love does not envy and does not make a vain display of its self. Does not boast. Does not behave its self unseemly, seeks not its own, is not easily provoked. Thinks no evil, rejoices not over iniquity but rejoices in the truth. Bears all things. Believes all things. Hopes all things, endures all things. Love never fails" (1 Corin. 13:4-8).

162

If you have love in your heart faith will also abide. If you have love in your heart favor will be upon you. If you have love in your heart, fear has no place in you and doubt is powerless. When the love of God abides in you there is God: "For you will know them by their love" (John 13:34). They will see everything coming from the hand of God, good or bad, and will strengthen you to give thanks in all things, because they know the will of God and desire his love above their own lives. For God is love; he is their life and they know that without him they would be miserably doomed.

As tiny as a seed is, so is God's love. Just as the seed holds inside of it all of its full potential to come forth and produce much fruit, so is the love of God in our hearts. What one day was small, as we begin to draw closer and closer to that which is within, that tiny seed begins to consume all of our attention and grow till one day our love for it becomes stronger and more solid than anything else. So Lord, we have need of you and without you we can do nothing.

Come, Lord Jesus, Come.

A SUPERNATURAL GOD

And God said, "Let there be light, and there was light."

—Genesis 1:3

But the angel said to her, "Do not be afraid, Mary, you have found favor with God. You will be with child and give birth to a son, and you are to give him the name Jesus. He will be great and will be called the Son of the Most High. The Lord God will give him the throne of his father David, and he will reign over the house of Jacob forever; his kingdom will never end." "How will this be?" Mary asked the angel, "since I am a virgin?"

—Luke 1:30-34

"Lord, if it's you," Peter replied, "tell me to come to you on the water." "Come," he said; then Peter got down out of the boat, walked on the water and came toward Jesus. But when he saw the wind, he was afraid and, beginning to sink, cried out, "Lord, save me!" Immediately Jesus reached out his hand and caught him. "You of little faith," he said, "why did you doubt?"

—Matthew 14:28-31

Many times in the Bible we see God's supernatural power demonstrated. In the beginning he established his power and dominance through creation; an act above and beyond anything that man could ever do. He speaks and light comes forth, heavens and earth come into existence, the birds of the air, the fish in the seas, the plants, and the animals come to be all at his command. Our very existence as man came forth at his spoken word and we live every day by his power. We see the sun rise and fall, we see the earth bring forth plants, and our own hearts beat because God wills it into existence. He is an Almighty God and many times we fail to acknowledge his awesome power and supernatural existence.

He does not have to conform to the laws of nature; he made everything that exists. It all belongs to him and he controls it all. He keeps the universe in balance and his intelligence is far greater than we could ever imagine. One day we will see, know, and truly understand. Until then we have incredible glimpses in his Word and in the world demonstrating his power, that we may come to know and trust this Almighty, supernatural God.

Moses was a man who stood before God to witness his ability to break the laws of nature on behalf of his servant and to demonstrate his power and great love toward his people. As Moses stood before the Red Sea, with all of the Israelites following him, and Pharaoh and his army pursuing them, he could not have imagined that the Red Sea would open up and allow a way of escape. But God commanded the waters to open up to save his people and the waters obeyed his command. To further demonstrate his love, he conquered the enemy by causing the waters to come together and drown Pharaoh's army.

Mary, a virgin girl was told she would give birth to a son who would be the Savior. She knew this was impossible according to man's standards, but she believed the words of God's angel and found favor with God. She supernaturally brought forth a child, the son of God. She had the faith to believe that God was almighty and could do what he said. She was willing to risk the humiliation she would face from those around her in order to obey. It appeared as if Mary was without virtue and her declaration of being with child and never having known a man had to have caused much disbelief with many who heard her words. Yet she was faithful and God proved himself to her because she believed.

Jesus, the son of God, was nailed to a cross and died. It appeared as if all was lost. It appeared as if he was a deceiver in deed and that his promises would die with him. But God who is eternal wanted to demonstrate his power and again broke the laws of nature. Three days in the grave and Jesus is brought back to life. And in his resurrection he further demonstrates his power and love toward his people. Even Jesus had to believe and trust himself to the Almighty God in the face of humiliation and dishonor. He knew that his father was The Almighty and would not let him remain in the grave.

So many times we see the amazing power of God in our everyday lives but fail to acknowledge that without him we could not even exist. We put limits on God and think he is not able to do certain things because we judge God according to natural laws and from our perspective. We fail to believe he is the creator of everything and nothing exists without his command. In knowing and acknowledging this we ought to have confidence that he is able to perfectly take care of us and deal with our situations. He truly is able to do anything yet we first must believe and completely trust him. We, like Moses will find ourselves in impossible situations facing our own personal dilemmas and it will seem as if there is no way out or no realistic answer to solve our problems. We need to put ourselves in the hands of an Almighty

God and look back through the pages of history and realize he is the same yesterday, today, and forever more. He can bend natural laws, time, and space. He can move mountains and scale walls on our behalf if we will step out in faith and trust him. Move beyond what our eyes can see and into eternity where our Father abides. Nothing is too hard for God.

Won't you trust him with that impossible situation? Won't you rely on an Almighty God, who alone knows the number of hairs on our head? Who, if we are willing to surrender and give up on our ideas and trust that he is able, will make a way and fix it for us. As Peter stepped out of the boat and began to approach Jesus on the water, so will we too have to get out of the boat and approach Jesus. Let us learn from Peter to keep our eyes on Jesus even when the wind

172

blows and the waves get stirred up. Let us expect our

God to move in a supernatural way on our behalf.

CAN'T I HAVE ANYTHING, LORD?

He who is concerned about his life shall lose it.

—Matthew 10:39

Enter in through the narrow gate. For wide is the gate and broad is the road that leads to destruction, and many enter through it. But small is the gate and narrow the road that leads to life and only a few find it.

—Matthew 7:13-14

He who wishes to follow me, let him deny himself, and take up his cross and follow me. For whoever wishes to save his life shall lose it; and whoever loses his life for my sake shall find it.

—Matthew 16:24-25

Concern: to be of importance; to have an influence on; to be a care, trouble, or distress to; marked interest or regard, arising through a personal tie or relationship, something that related or belongs to one; matter of consideration; interest, engaged, regarding.

There have been times when God's hand has been on me to lead me down his path and I've cried out to him, "Can't I have anything, Lord?" Typically in those times he does not seem to respond to my cries. I know he is there, yet not in the way I want him to be. I want him to come in and fix everything so I can be at ease again. I cry and cry and he stands by waiting for me to get it. Slowly, late in the midnight hour, my heart reveals to me my most dreaded fear: Death.

My attachment to the world is being exposed and he is trying to bring about deliverance in my life. Does he care about the pain I am in? Yes, he does. Remember Jesus too was tempted at all points just as we are; he has shared in our struggles. He knows us intimately, even better than we know ourselves. He does desire to fix the situation; however, his ways are

177

not like our ways. We cry out to him to change the situation, but what we should really say is, "God have mercy on me and deliver me from my bondage of self and this world. Help me, Lord Jesus." We look to the situation and determine what is wrong; if in those times we would humbly turn toward a loving Savior, we would find the problem is with us. Yes, we may be mistreated. Yes, maybe it seems as if the devil has cut lose in our circumstances and situations. Yes, we do have to suffer and will be persecuted, but God uses all these hard times and difficult trials to teach us how to be like him.

Remember before you and I came into the knowledge of Christ and before we heard his voice, we were wayward and deep in our sins. Yet he remained firm and unshaken in his love for us. He looked

178

through the eyes of eternity, seeing us in him, knowing all of our days and all the struggles and stumbling we would go through. Still he remained firm in his love. He didn't waver when we were covered with filth; no, he loved us. And he wants us to do the same: "Be ye therefore perfect, as your Father in heaven is perfect" (Matt. 5:48).

In my tears and times of trial, it seems hard to understand God. Yes, he cares about what we go through. Our Father loves us and only he knows what is best. Yes, we do have many hardships and the walk with Christ is one of not always knowing; it is the Holy Spirit, faith, hope, and love that pull us through. It is difficult to want things out of life, our hearts desires, especially when they seem a million miles away. These are things God has promised, yet they are the very

things that look and seem impossible. They may even

break and shatter before us. All the while the toiling

within could make you scream. He is there in the midst

of it all. He is teaching us to not be concerned about

our lives; we are to concern ourselves with Him.

Deny ourselves, take up our cross, knowing

that taking up the cross leads to a road of pain,

suffering, and death. Yes, death, but only to the parts

of our old man that are still alive. We will and do gain

life, his life by leaving behind our lives. It is life in

abundance, his everlasting life; a life of peace and

reconciliation with the Father. In those times of trial

remember there is no resurrection lest there first be a

death. There is no joy without some sorrow. Jesus

loves us much that he chose to suffer and give his life

180

as a sacrifice for the sake of many. When we suffer ourselves for the kingdom of God, we do it for the sake of others. God wants us to stop looking at ourselves and look through the eyes that see from eternity.

Don't become hard-hearted when the pressure is on and when the world hates you. Overcome the world; love, be patient, and kind. Acknowledge God and trust in him. He will give you the desires of your heart. Wait upon the Lord, trust in him, and he shall bring your heart's desires to pass. Don't give up and don't look to the world, it will only bring more heartache and trouble. Willingly give him your heart in every situation. I know it gets hard. He said, "How difficult is the road which leads to life and few are found on it" (Matt. 7:14).

Few are found on it because it does take everything you want away at times. God may give these things back to you once they have been purified and in his time, if he promised it, he will give them to you. He may only remove these things for a season in order that he might clear us of our attachment to them and that we may love him more than anything. There will be times you will not get what you think you want and need so badly, but the question remains, what will your response toward God be? Prayerfully, I hope you and I will say, "Lord, you are enough for me; I am satisfied with you."

www.ingramcontent.com/pod-product-compliance
Lightning Source LLC
Chambersburg PA
CBHW060013050426
42448CB00012B/2732